THE EXODUS

Activity Book for Beginners

The Exodus Activity Book for Beginners

Bible Pathway Adventures® is a trademark of BPA Publishing Ltd.
Defenders of the Faith® is a trademark of BPA Publishing Ltd.

ISBN: 978-1-98-858597-0

Author: Pip Reid
Creative Director: Curtis Reid

For free Bible resources including coloring pages, worksheets, puzzles and more, visit our website at:

www.biblepathwayadventures.com

 # Introduction for Parents

Enjoy teaching your children about the Bible with *The Exodus Activity Book for Beginners*. Packed with detailed lesson plans, coloring pages, fun worksheets, and puzzles to help educators just like you teach children the Biblical faith. PLUS, scripture references for easy Bible verse look-up. The perfect discipleship tool for Sabbath and Sunday School teachers, and homeschooling.

Bible Pathway Adventures helps educators teach children the Biblical faith in a fun and creative way. We do this via our storybooks, Activity Books, and printable activities - available for download on our website www.biblepathwayadventures.com

Thanks for buying this Activity Book and supporting our ministry. Every book purchased helps us continue our work providing free Classroom Packs and discipleship resources to missions and families around the world.

The search for Truth is more fun than Tradition!

★BONUS★

Our illustrated The Exodus storybook is available for download.
Type the link into your browser to get your FREE copy today!
https://BookHip.com/MKSJFX

 # Table of Contents

© BPA Publishing Ltd 2020

LESSON 1 | **Lesson Plan**
Red Sea crossing

Teacher: _____

Today's Bible passages: Exodus 13:17-22 and 14:19-29

 Welcome prayer:
Pray a simple prayer with the children before you begin the lesson.

Lesson objectives:
In this lesson, children will learn:
1. How God led the Israelites through the desert
2. How God saved the Israelites from the Egyptians

Did You Know?
Explorers have found old Egyptian chariot wheels and animal skeletons at the bottom of the Gulf of Aqaba.

Bible lesson overview:
The Israelites followed Moses out of Egypt. God used a tall cloud during the day and a pillar of fire at night to show them the way to go. Soon they reached the Red Sea. Meanwhile, the king of Egypt was angry the Israelites were gone. He sent his army to chase after them. When the Israelites saw the army, they were scared. But God opened up the water so they could walk along dry ground to the other side of the Red Sea. When the Egyptians did the same thing, the water crashed down on them and they all drowned. The Israelites were safe!

Let's Review:

Questions to ask your students:

1. How did God show Moses the way to the Red Sea?
2. Do you think the Israelites scared? Why / Why not?
3. How did God part the Red Sea?
4. How did the Israelites get to the other side of the Red Sea?
5. What happened to the Egyptians when they tried to cross the Red Sea?

 A memory verse to help children remember God's Word:

…the Israelites went through the sea on dry ground." (Exodus 14:29)

Activities:

Connect the dots: Moses
Worksheet: God's plan for Moses
Coloring page: Leaving Egypt…
Worksheet: Day and night
Let's learn Hebrew: matzah
Color 'n trace: The king of Egypt
Bible activity: Dress like an Israelite
Worksheet: Trace the words
Red Sea crossing game: Help the Israelites cross the Red Sea
Worksheet: What's in the sea?
Worksheet: Song of Moses

  **Closing prayer:**

End the lesson with a small prayer.

🌿 Moses 🌿

Moses was the leader of the Israelites (Exodus 14:1).
Connect the dots to see the picture.

God's plan for
Moses

Moses was born in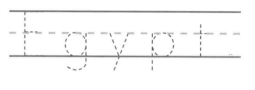
He was a Hebrew.

Moses asked ___Pharaoh___
to free the Hebrews.

Pharaoh told the ___Hebrews___
to leave Egypt.

Leaving Egypt

The children of Israel left the land of Egypt
with their unbaked bread (Exodus 12:34-39).
Draw a sun in the sky. Color the picture.

Day and night

God led the children of Israel with a pillar of cloud by day, and a pillar of fire by night (Exodus 13:21). Draw the pillars below.

Day

Night

✦ Matzah ✦

The Hebrew word for unleavened bread is matzah. Matzah is a type of bread made with flour and water. The Hebrews left Egypt during the seven-day Feast of Unleavened Bread.

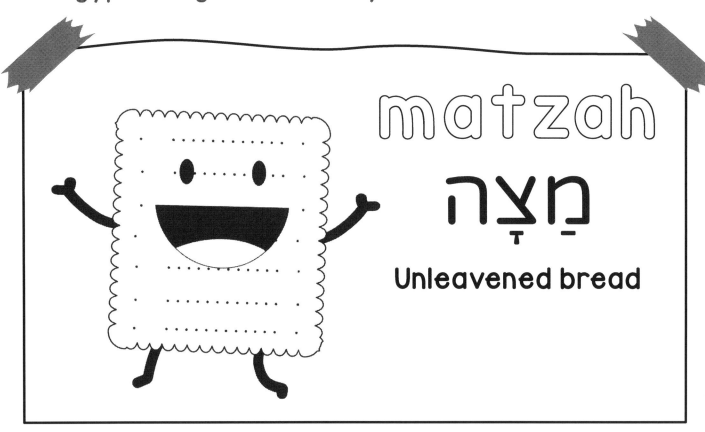

matzah

מַצָּה

Unleavened bread

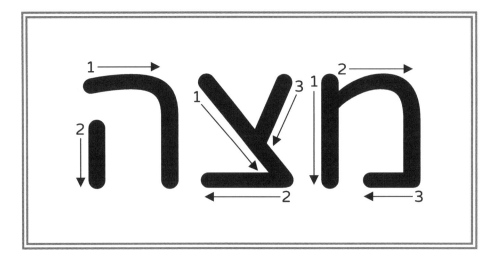

Let's write!

Write the word 'matzah' on the lines below.

מצה

Try this on your own.
Remember that Hebrew is read from RIGHT to LEFT.

The king of Egypt

Pharaoh was the king of Egypt (Exodus 12:29).
Trace the words. Color the picture.

The king of Egypt

Dress like an Israelite

The ancient Israelites wore clothing like tunics and robes. Let's make a tunic! Ask your parents to help you do this.

Instructions:

1. Parents - measure your child's body from elbow to elbow and knee to shoulder.
2. Find an old blanket or sheet as big as your child and fold it in half.
3. Cut a slit in the middle of the fold wide enough to fit their head.
4. Place the 'tunic' over their head. Tie a belt made from rope, ribbon, leather, or cloth around their waist.

1.   2.   3.   4.

ta-da!

Trace the Words

Color the pictures.

Help the Israelites
cross the Red Sea

Ask children questions about the lesson.
When they answer correctly, they can color a square and
move through the Red Sea until they reach the other side.

What's in the sea?

The children of Israel went through the sea on dry ground.
Pharaoh's chariots and horses and men chased after them
(Exodus 14:28-30). Color what belongs in the sea.

Song of Moses

(Exodus 15:1-4)

I will sing to God

He has done great things.

He threw horse and rider

into the sea.

God is my strength.

He saves me,

and I sing songs of praise to him.

He is my God and I praise him.

LESSON 2 | Lesson Plan
The ten commandments

Teacher: _____

Today's Bible passages: Exodus 19:10-20 and 20:1-20

Welcome prayer:
Pray a simple prayer with the children before you begin the lesson.

Lesson objectives:
In this lesson, children will learn:
1. How God gave the Israelites the ten commandmentss
2. The ten commandments

Did You Know?
A shofar is a trumpet made from a ram's horn.

Bible lesson overview:
The Israelites walked to a mountain called Sinai and set up camp. God said to Moses, "Get everyone ready. On the third day I will come down on this mountain." On the third day, God covered the mountain in cloud. There was thunder and lightning, and loud shofar (trumpet) blasts. It was very noisy! Moses took the Israelites out of the camp so God could speak to them. There He gave them the ten commandments. When everyone saw the thunder and lightning, and heard the shofar blasts, they were afraid. Moses said to them, "Don't be scared. God has come to test you."

Let's Review:

Questions to ask your students:

1. What was the name of the mountain?
2. What happened on the third day?
3. How many commandments did God give the Israelites that day?
4. Why were the Israelites afraid?
5. What did Moses tell the Israelites?

 A memory verse to help children remember God's Word:

"Honor your mother and father." (Exodus 20:12)

Activities:

Finish the picture: Mount Sinai
Bible word search puzzle: Mount Sinai
Let's learn Hebrew: shofar
Coloring page: The ten commandments
Math activity: The number ten
Bible activity: Place the Israelites inside the tent
Bible craft: Help Moses climb Mount Sinai
Bible craft: The ten commandments
Worksheet: Do you keep the commandments?
Memory verse: Honor your father and mother
Puzzle: Who spoke to the Israelites?
Worksheet: T is for tribe

 Closing prayer:

End the lesson with a small prayer.

 Mount Sinai

Draw cloud and lightning on the mountain.
Draw the people at the bottom of the mountain.

🌿 Mount Sinai 🌿

The Israelites camped near Mount Sinai (Exodus 19:2).
Find and circle each of the words from the list below.

```
T E N G T C
S T A O E A
X W W D N M
P N C S T P
S H O F A R
F I R E L J
```

FIRE   TENT
TEN   GOD
SHOFAR   CAMP

✦ Shofar ✦

The Hebrew word for trumpet is shofar. A shofar is made from a ram's horn. When the Israelites heard the shofar blast, they were scared! (Exodus 20:18)

shofar

שׁוֹפָר

trumpet

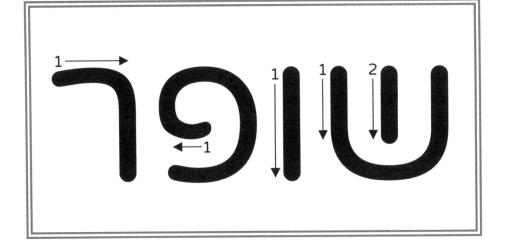

Let's write!

Practice writing this Hebrew word on the lines below.

שׁופר

שׁופר

Try this on your own.
Remember that Hebrew is read from RIGHT to LEFT.

The Ten Commandments

God spoke the ten commandments
to the Israelites.

10 10 10 10 10

Write the number ten in the boxes below.

How many fingers are there?

Do you obey the ten commandments?

....

Do you keep the commandments?

 **1** I am Yahweh.
No other gods

 **2** Do not make idols

 **3** Do not misuse God's name

 **4** Rest on the Sabbath

 **5** Honor your father and mother

 **6** Do not murder

 **7** No adultery

 **8** Do not steal

 **9** Do not lie

 **10** Do not want your neighbor's things

"Honor your mother and father."

(Exodus 20:12)

Who spoke to the Israelites?

Fill in the blanks using the chart below. What do you see?

Who spoke
the Ten
Commandments?

$\overline{7}$ $\overline{15}$ $\overline{4}$ $\overline{19}$ $\overline{16}$ $\overline{15}$ $\overline{11}$ $\overline{5}$

$\overline{20}$ $\overline{15}$ $\overline{20}$ $\overline{8}$ $\overline{5}$

$\overline{16}$ $\overline{5}$ $\overline{15}$ $\overline{16}$ $\overline{12}$ $\overline{5}$

A	B	C	D	E	F	G	H	I	J	K	L	M
1	2	3	4	5	6	7	8	9	10	11	12	13
N	O	P	Q	R	S	T	U	V	W	X	Y	Z
14	15	16	17	18	19	20	21	22	23	24	25	26

T is for tribe

A tribe is a big group of people. They are usually from the same family. There are 12 tribes of Israel (Exodus 39:14). Trace the letters and word. Color the picture.

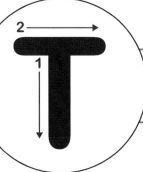

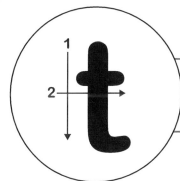

Trace the letter t

Color the banner.

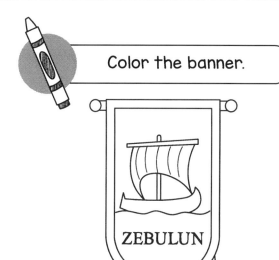

ZEBULUN

LESSON 3 | Lesson Plan
The golden calf

Teacher: _____

Today's Bible passage: Exodus 32:1-20

Welcome prayer:
Pray a simple prayer with the children before you begin the lesson.

Lesson objectives:
In this lesson, children will learn:
1. Why Aaron made a golden calf
2. How Moses destroyed the golden calf

Did You Know?
An idol is something we think is more important than God.

Bible lesson overview:
While Moses was on Mount Sinai, the Israelites asked Aaron to make them an idol. They gave Aaron their gold jewelry and he made them a golden calf. The Israelites were happy! They had a big party to celebrate. But God was not happy. "Let me destroy these people," He said. Moses begged God not to do this and God agreed. Then Moses ran back down the mountain to the camp. When he saw the golden calf, he was so angry that he smashed the two stone tablets on the ground (on which were written the Ten Commandments). After he burned the calf in the fire, he ground it to dust and poured it in the water for the people to drink.

Let's Review:

Questions to ask your students:

1. What did the people ask Aaron to make?
2. Where was Moses while Aaron made the golden calf?
3. What did God say when He saw what the people had done?
4. Why do you think Moses smashed the two stone tablets on the ground?
5. What did Moses do with the golden calf?

 A memory verse to help children remember God's Word:

"Moses destroyed the calf.." (Exodus 32:20)

Activities:

Worksheet: C is for calf
Labyrinth: Moses to the rescue
Bible craft: The golden calf
Bible activity: Aaron makes a gold calf
Color 'n trace: Aaron
Worksheet: Gold, gold, gold!
Worksheet: Moses' anger
Worksheet: Moses burns the calf
Worksheet: What's different?
Worksheet: Scavenger Hunt
Bible flashcards: The Exodus
Worksheet: What a lot of quail!
Worksheet: Matching pairs

 Closing prayer:

End the lesson with a small prayer.

C is for calf

The Israelites made a golden calf to worship God (Exodus 32:1-6). Trace the letter and words. Color the picture.

C

Calf

c is for calf

 Moses to the rescue!

Help Moses get down Mount Sinai to stop the Israelites worshipping a golden calf.

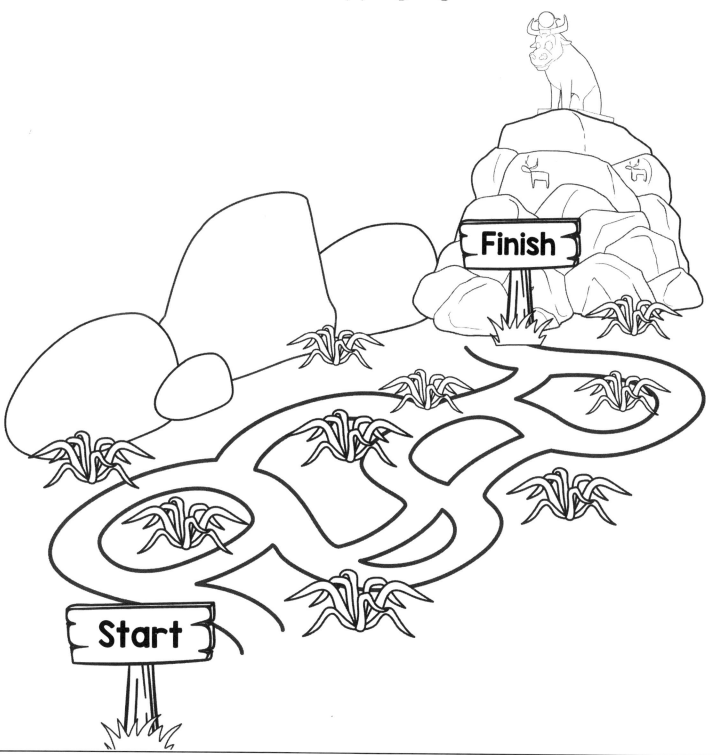

Aaron

Aaron made a gold calf for the Israelites
(Exodus 32:4). Trace the name. Color the picture.

Aaron

Gold, gold, gold!

Aaron used the Israelites' gold earrings to make a gold calf (Exodus 32:2-4). Trace along the dotted lines. Circle the biggest object.

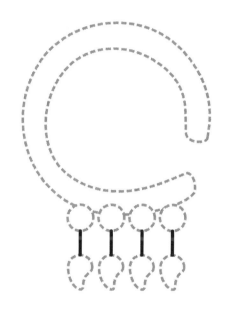

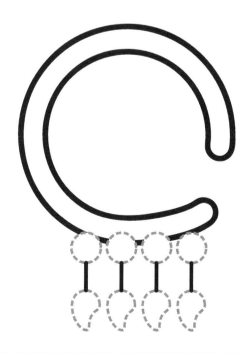

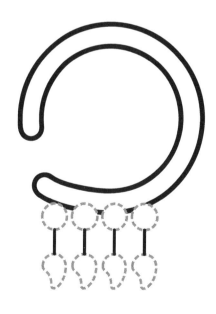

🌿 Moses' anger 🌿

When Moses saw the gold calf and the people dancing, he was angry! He broke the tablets into pieces (Exodus 32:19). Draw Moses' angry face in the space below. Why do you think Moses was angry?

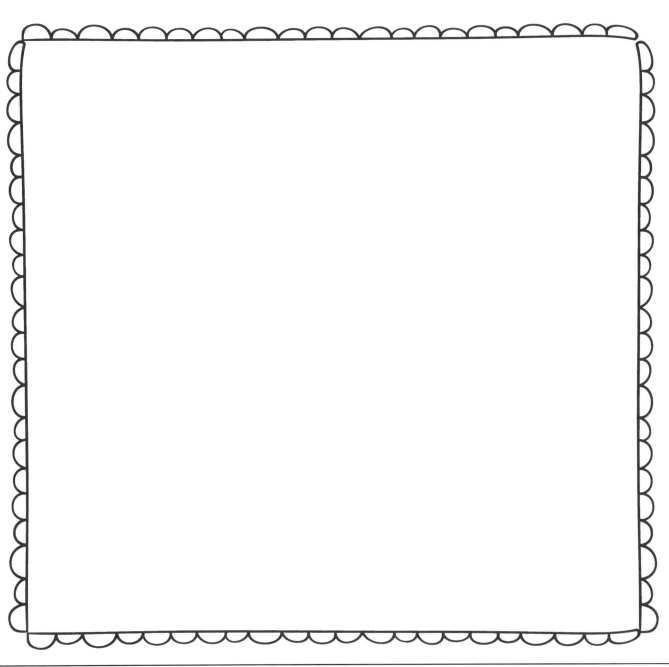

Moses burns the calf

The Israelites' made a golden calf. Moses was not happy.
He burned the calf with fire (Exodus 32:20).
Use the color code to finish the picture.

1 = brown	2 = yellow	3 = orange	4 = red

www.biblepathwayadventures.com
The Exodus Activity Book (Beginners)

© BPA Publishing Ltd 2020

What's different?

Circle the picture that is different.

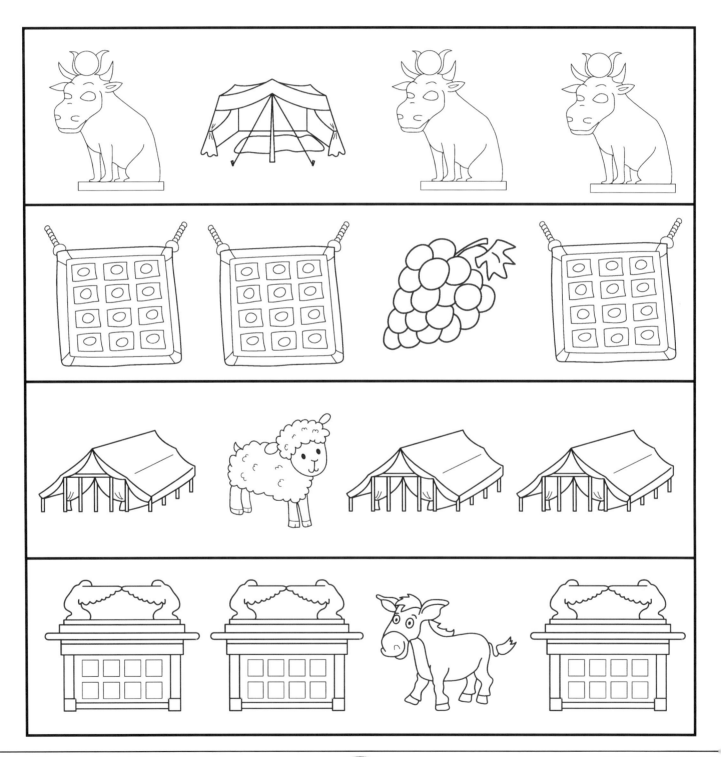

❧ Scavenger Hunt ❧

The Israelites lived in tents for forty years.
What items did they need? Ask children to find these
items around their home or classroom. Discuss
how the Israelites may have used each item.

bowl

tent

pillow

water bottle

mat

tent peg

cup

🌿 What a lot of quail! 🌿

While the Israelites lived in the wilderness, they ate lots of quail meat. Count the birds and write the number in the box.

Matching pairs

Draw a line between the matching objects.
Color the matching objects the same way.

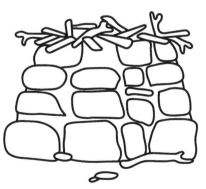

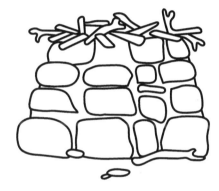

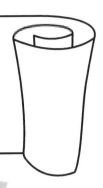

LESSON 4 | Lesson Plan
The tabernacle

Teacher: _____

Today's Bible passage: Exodus 35:4-29

Welcome prayer:
Pray a simple prayer with the children before you begin the lesson.

Lesson objectives:
In this lesson, children will learn:
1. The purpose of the tabernacle
2. How Moses gathered items to build the tabernacle

Did You Know?
The tabernacle and its courtyard would fit into half a football field.

Bible lesson overview:
God told Moses to build a special tent called a tabernacle. This was a place where He could live among the people. Moses needed many things to build the tabernacle so he asked everyone to help. Some people brought gold and silver, others brought wood, fabric, and animal skins. They gave Moses so many things that he had to tell them to stop giving! Afterwards, they built the tabernacle just how God had told them. Everyone who was skilled or had a special talent (like builders or sewers) helped build the tabernacle.

Let's Review:

Questions to ask your students:

1. What did God ask Moses to do?
2. What was the purpose of the tabernacle?
3. What did Moses ask everyone to do?
4. What gifts did the people bring Moses to build the tabernacle?
5. Why did Moses tell the people to stop giving?

 A memory verse to help children remember God's Word:

"God loves a cheerful giver." (2 Corinthians 9:7)

Activities:

Color 'n trace: The tabernacle
Complete the pattern
Bible activity: Place the items inside the tabernacle
Worksheet: A is for ark
Worksheet: Ark of the covenant
Alphabet worksheet: G is for gold
Bible craft: The tabernacle
Worksheet: Camp of Israel
Coloring page: God loves a cheerful giver
Worksheet: The number two
Worksheet: What's my sound?
Worksheet: O is for olive

 Closing prayer:
End the lesson with a small prayer.

🌿 The tabernacle 🌿

God asked Moses to build the tabernacle.
Trace the word. Color the picture.

The tabernacle

A is for ark

The ten commandments were kept inside a gold box called the ark of the covenant. Trace the letter and words. Color the picture.

a

ark

a is for ark

🌿 Ark of the covenant 🌿

The ark was a box covered in gold. It was kept inside the tabernacle. The ten commandments were written on tablets inside the ark. Draw two tablets inside the ark.

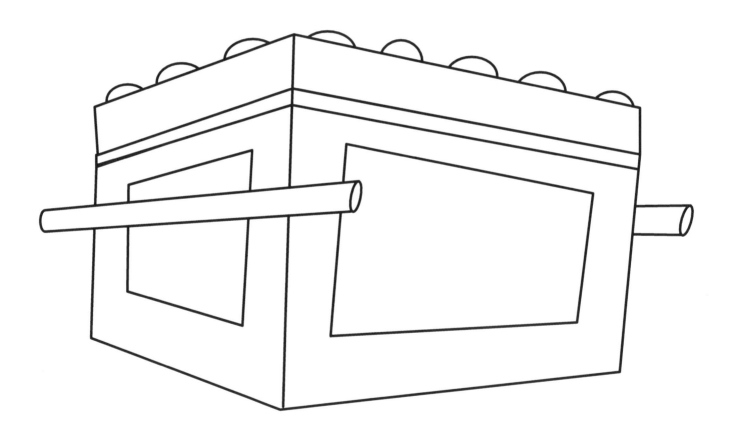

🌿 Camp of Israel 🌿

God told the 12 tribes of Israel to camp around the tabernacle (Numbers 2). Can you write the name of each tribe inside an empty box?

Zebulun	Naphtali	Manasseh	Simeon
Judah	Dan	Ephraim	Reuben
Issachar	Asher	Benjamin	Gad

🌿 G is for gold 🌿

The Israelites gave Moses lots of gold to build the tabernacle. Trace the letters. Color the picture.

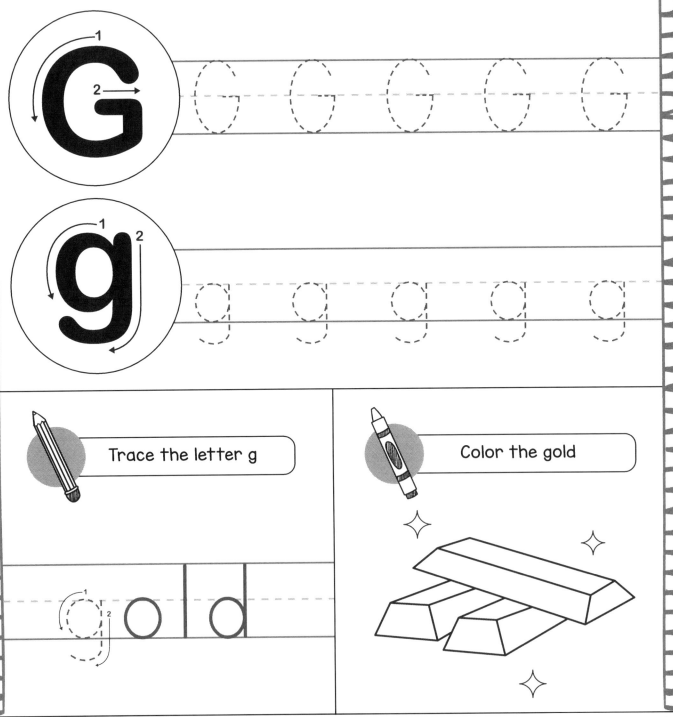

Trace the letter g

Color the gold

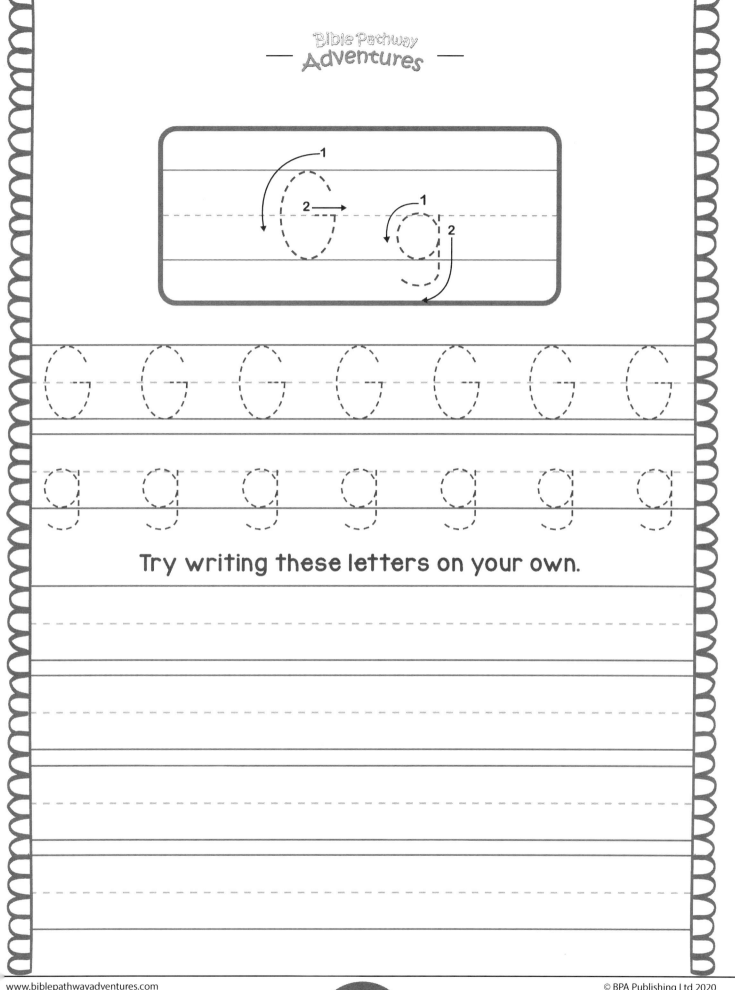

Try writing these letters on your own.

"God loves a cheerful giver."

(2 Corinthians 9:7)

HOLY BIBLE

The number two

There were two altars in the tabernacle; the altar of incense and the altar of burnt offering.
Write the number two. Color the pictures.

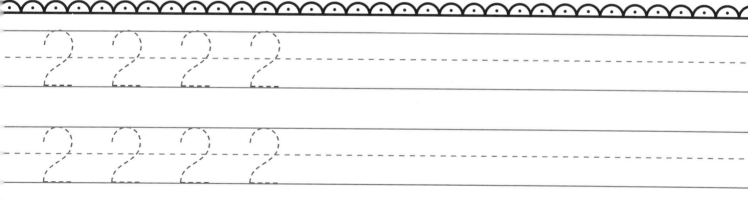

🌿 What's my sound? 🌿

The word 'menorah' starts with the letter M. Circle and color the pictures that have the same beginning sound as menorah.

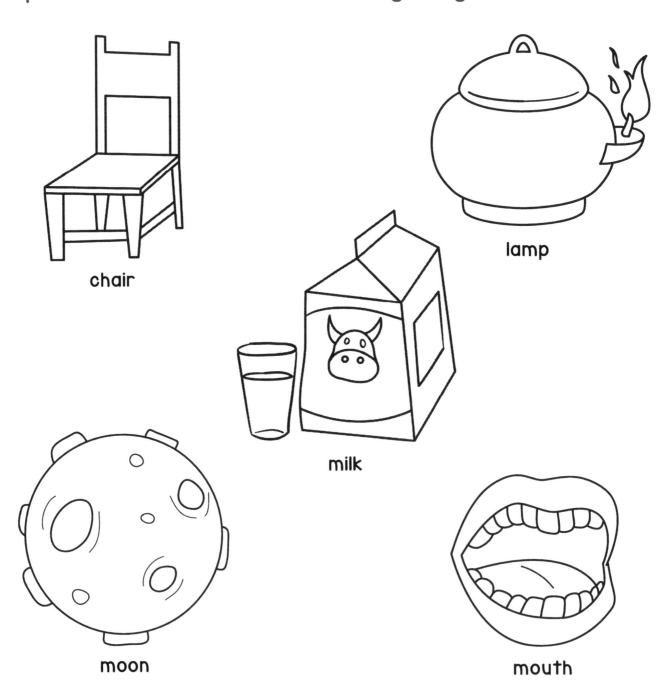

chair

lamp

milk

moon

mouth

 # O is for olive

Olive oil is made from olives. Olives grow on trees.
The priests used olive oil to light the menorah (lampstand)
in the tabernacle. Trace along the dotted lines to add
more olives to the branch. Count the olives!

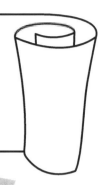

LESSON 5 | Lesson Plan
Spies into Canaan

Teacher: _____

Today's Bible passage: Numbers 13:1-33

Welcome prayer:
Pray a simple prayer with the children before you begin the lesson.

Lesson objectives:
In this lesson, children will learn:
1. How Moses chose twelve men (spies) to visit the land of Canaan
2. What the spies saw when they visited the land of Canaan

Did You Know?
Joshua became the leader of the Israelites after Moses died.

Bible lesson overview:
God told the Israelites He would give them the Promised Land. He said to Moses, "Send twelve men to explore the land of Canaan." So, Moses chose one leader from each of the twelve tribes of Israel. The men went to the land of Canaan for 40 days. They were in for a big surprise! The fruit was big, the cities were big, and some people were as tall as cedar trees. They couldn't believe their eyes! When they came back to the camp, ten of the spies said to Moses, "Giant people live in the land. We were like grasshoppers to them. We cannot fight them." Only two spies - Joshua and Caleb – believed what God had said.

Let's Review:

Questions to ask your students:

1. How did Moses choose the spies?
2. How many tribes of Israel are there?
3. How long were the spies in the land of Canaan?
4. What did the spies see in the land of Canaan?
5. Which two spies trusted God?

 A memory verse to help children remember God's Word:

"We felt like little grasshoppers." (Numbers 13:33)

 Activities:

Worksheet: G is for giant
Worksheet: I spy!
Bible coloring: Twelve tribes of Israel
Bible craft: Spies into Canaan
Bible word search puzzle: Spies into Canaan
Bible craft: Spy out the land of Canaan
Worksheet: Who do you trust?
Color 'n Trace: Fruit in the land of Canaan
Labyrinth: Spies into Canaan
Coloring page: The promised land
Worksheet: Trace the words
Certificate of award

 Closing prayer:

End the lesson with a small prayer.

✦ G is for Giant ✦

When the spies reached the land of Canaan,
they saw giant men called Nephilim. Trace the letter
and words. Color the picture.

g

giant

g is for giant

❧ I spy! ❧

The spies saw different kinds of fruit in the land of Canaan.
Color the same fruit a single color. Then count each type of
fruit and write the number on the label.

🌿 Twelve Tribes of Israel 🌿

The high priest wore a special breastplate with 12 gemstones. On each gemstone was written the name of a tribe of Israel (Exodus 28:21). Color the picture.

🌿 Spies into Canaan 🌿

Moses sent 12 men to the land of Canaan.
Find and circle each of the words from the list below.

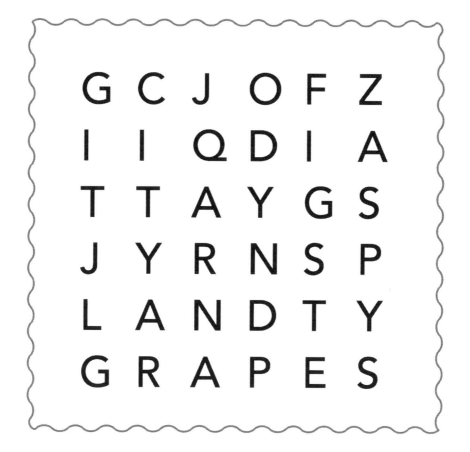

```
G C J O F Z
I I Q D I A
T T A Y G S
J Y R N S P
L A N D T Y
G R A P E S
```

GIANT   FIGS

GRAPES   SPY

CITY   LAND

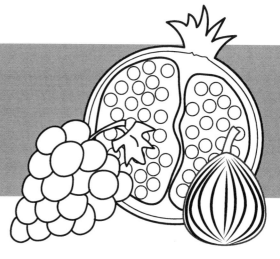

www.biblepathwayadventures.com
The Exodus Activity Book (Beginners)

Spy out the land of Canaan!

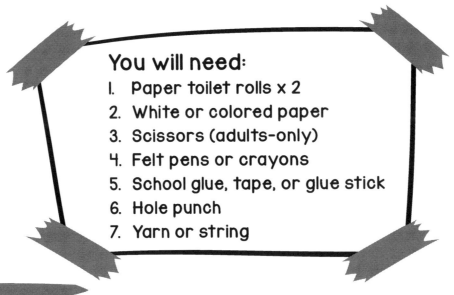

You will need:
1. Paper toilet rolls x 2
2. White or colored paper
3. Scissors (adults-only)
4. Felt pens or crayons
5. School glue, tape, or glue stick
6. Hole punch
7. Yarn or string

Instructions:

1. Paste a piece of white or colored paper around each toilet roll.
2. Ask your child to decorate each toilet roll.
3. Tape the two rolls together using a piece of tape at each end.
4. Create a hole in the outer side of each tube. Thread yarn or string through to create a neck strap.

1.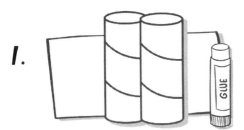

2.

3.

4.   ta-da!

Who do you trust?

Joshua and Caleb trusted God. When you trust God,
you know He will do what He says. Who do you trust?
Write their names in the boxes below.

Spies into Canaan

Help the spies make their way to the land of Canaan.

The promised land

Draw two spies carrying a bunch of giant grapes to complete the picture.

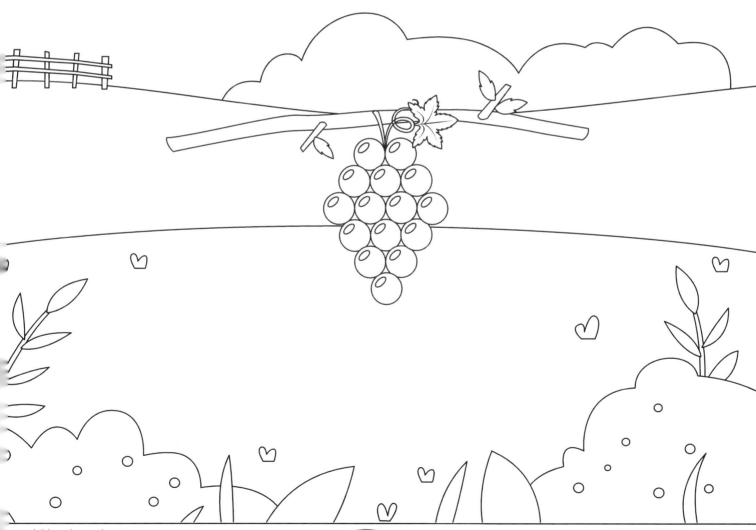

Trace the Words

Color the pictures.

CRAFTS & PROJECTS

© BPA Publishing Ltd 2020

🌿 The Israelites 🌿

The Israelites camped near Mount Sinai (Exodus 19:2).
Color and cut out the people. Paste them inside the tent.

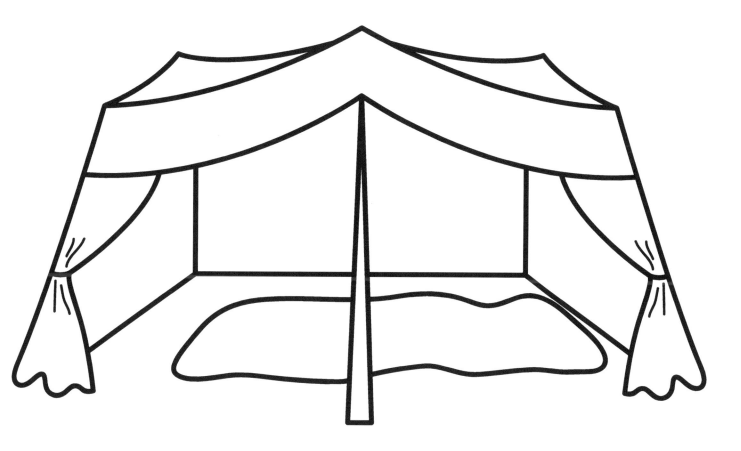

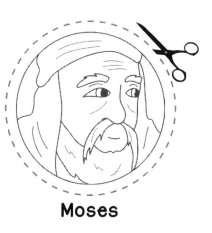

Moses

Israelite

Israelite

Help Moses climb Mount Sinai

You will need:
1. Paper plate (one for each child)
2. Paper fastener (one for each plate)
3. Paint, markers, or crayons
4. Scissors (adults-only)

Instructions:

1. Cut your paper plate in half.
2. Color your mountain grey using paint, markers or crayons. Draw green trees or leaves at the bottom of the plate.
3. Cut out the Moses template on the next page.
4. Insert the paper fastener into the bottom center of the paper plate. Push the fastener into the long end of the Moses template and secure. Now Moses can climb up and down Mount Sinai!

1.   *2.*   *3.*

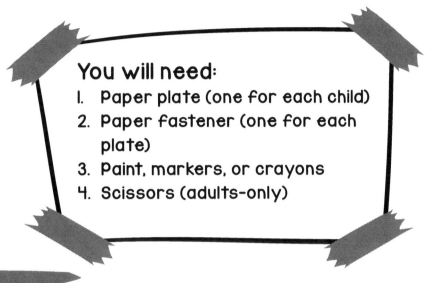

ta-da!

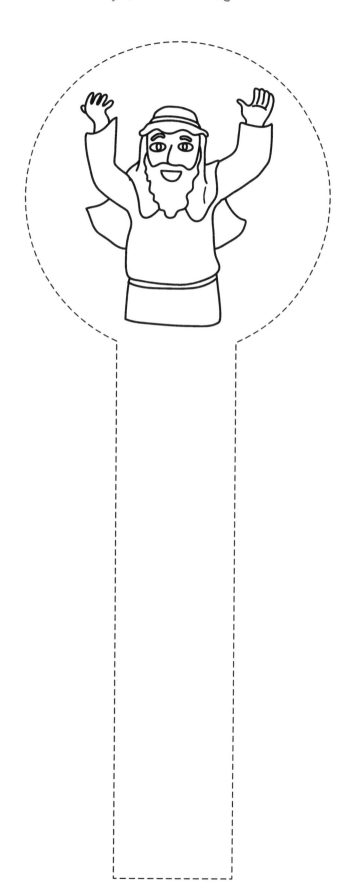

Ten commandments craft

You will need:
1. Heavy card stock
2. Scissors (adults-only)
3. Crayons, paint, or colored pencils
4. School glue
5. Jumbo craft sticks

Instructions:

1. Color the ten numbers and cut out. Paste onto heavy card stock.
2. Option 1: Glue a jumbo craft stick to the back of each number. Help your children to write the correct number on each craft stick.
3. Option 2: Help your children learn numbers 1-10 by asking them to match a colored number with a black & white number.

1.

2.

3.

ta-da!

Worship only God **1**

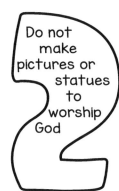
Do not make pictures or statues to worship God **2**

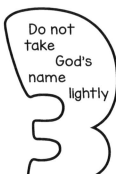
Do not take God's name lightly **3**

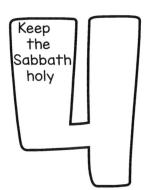
Keep the Sabbath holy **4**

Honor your parents **5**

Do not murder **6**

Do not commit adultery **7**

Do not steal **8**

Do not lie **9**

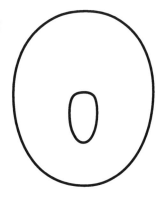
Do not desire other people's things **10**

Golden Calf craft

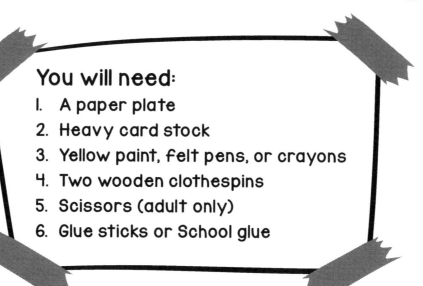

You will need:

1. A paper plate
2. Heavy card stock
3. Yellow paint, felt pens, or crayons
4. Two wooden clothespins
5. Scissors (adult only)
6. Glue sticks or School glue

Instructions:

1. Copy or print out the calf template on the next page. Paste onto heavy card stock. Have your child color it yellow.
2. Cut out the calf head.
3. Color the bottom of a paper plate yellow. Fold it in half and put two clothes pins at the bottom for its feet.
4. Paste the calf head to the right side of the paper plate.

1.    **2.**    **3.**    **4.**

ta-da!

Aaron makes a gold calf

Aaron made a calf out of gold for the Israelites
(Exodus 32:4). Color and cut out the people.
Place them around the calf.

Aaron

Israelite

Israelite

🌿 Flashcards 🌿

Color and cut out the flashcards.
Tape them around your house or classroom!

calf 1

sheep 2

tribes 3

tent 4

tablets

5

ark

6

grapes

7

altar

8

Complete the pattern

Cut out the objects and place them in the correct box.

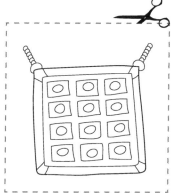

The tabernacle

Color and cut out the priest and objects.
Glue them inside the tabernacle.

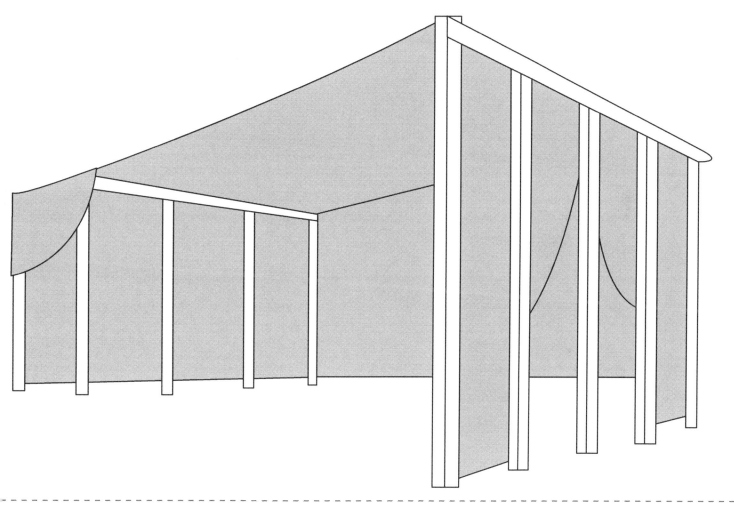

High Priest

ark of the covenant

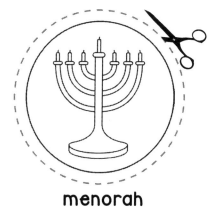

menorah

The tabernacle craft

You will need:
1. Scissors (adults-only)
2. Crayons, felt pens, or colored pencils
3. School glue

Instructions:

1. Copy or print out the template on the next page.
2. Color and cut out the tabernacle objects.
3. Paste each object inside the correct square on the template.

1.   2.   3.

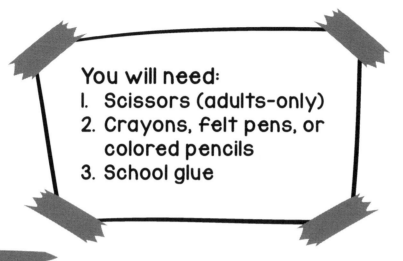

ta-da!

menorah	table of showbread	ark

altar	basin	altar of burnt offering

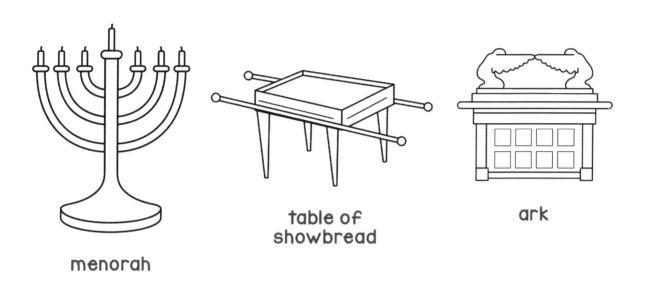

menorah

table of
showbread

ark

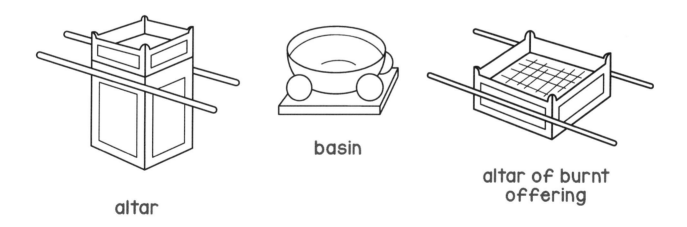

altar

basin

altar of burnt
offering

Spies into Canaan craft

You will need:

1. Heavy card stock or construction paper
2. Paint, felt pens, or crayons
3. Scissors (adult only)
4. Extra-strength glue sticks or tape

Instructions:

1. Color each puppet.
2. Paste the activity sheets onto pieces of cardboard or construction paper, and wait for the glue to dry.
3. Carefully cut out each of the puppets.
4. Wrap each puppet tab around your children's fingers, and tape.

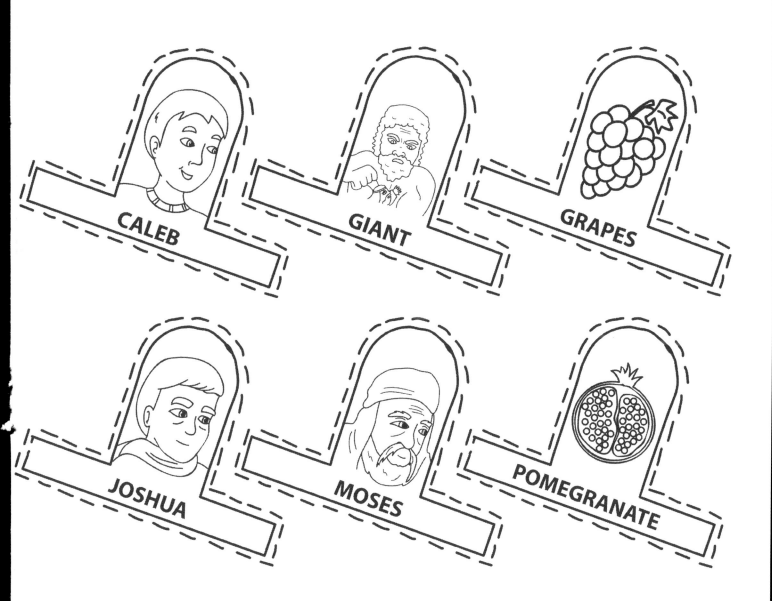

CALEB

GIANT

GRAPES

JOSHUA

MOSES

POMEGRANATE

Fruit in the land of Canaan

The spies showed Moses the fruit from Canaan.
Color and cut out the fruit to fill the bowl.

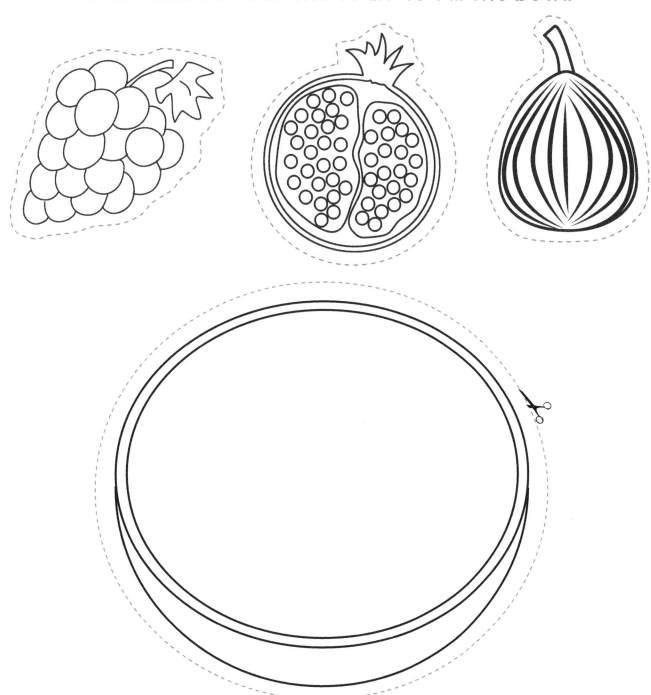

✿ Certificate of Award ✿

Certificate of Award

Congratulations

- -

For

- -

- - - - - - - - - - - - - - -

Signed

ANSWER KEY

LESSON ONE: Red Sea crossing
Let's Review answers:
1. Pillars of fire and cloud
2. Allow children to answer this question
3. God made the water split into two parts
4. The Israelites walked along the bottom of the sea on dry ground
5. The Egyptians drowned

LESSON TWO: The ten commandments
Let's Review answers:
1. Mount Sinai
2. There was thunder and lightning and loud shofars blasting. God spoke the ten commandments
3. Ten commandments
4. They saw the thunder, lightning, and heard the shofars and God's voice
5. "Don't be scared. God has come to test you."

LESSON THREE: The golden calf
Let's Review answers:
1. A god (golden calf)
2. Mount Sinai
3. He threated to destroy the Israelites
4. He was angry with the Israelites
5. He burned it, ground it to dust, and threw the gold dust in the water for the Israelites to drink

LESSON FOUR: The tabernacle
Let's Review answers:
1. Build a tabernacle
2. So that God could dwell among them
3. Bring gifts to build the tabernacle
4. Precious metals (gold, silver, bronze), fabric, wood, and animal hides
5. Moses had enough materials to build the tabernacle

LESSON FIVE: Spies into Canaan
Let's Review answers:
1. Moses chose one spy from each tribe of Israel
2. Twelve tribes
3. Forty days
4. Big fruit and giants
5. Joshua and Caleb

Discover more Activity Books!

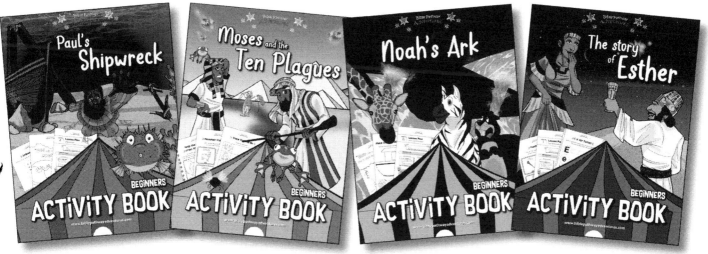

Available for purchase at www.biblepathwayadventures.com

INSTANT DOWNLOAD!

The Exodus
Twelve Tribes of Israel
Birth of the King
The Story of Joseph

Paul's Shipwreck
Moses Ten Plagues
Noah's Ark
The Story of Esther

Made in the USA
Columbia, SC
06 August 2022